PENINSULA 1

The object of this collection of drawings is interesting items of the local scene and to ... . ____ , the walker, the cyclist or the motorist. Secondly because the Peninsula was neglected, even avoided, for one hundred and fifty years or so it caused a general impression that there was a dull and dangerous area of no account in "The Garden of England". This impression also caused the idea that if some physically unpleasant looking or obnoxious smelling industry had to be found a place, who would notice it on the Hoo Peninsula? So it is time that some further effort is made to encourage more visitors who would, in turn, having tasted the unique qualities of the area, help to defend it against too great an encroachment of development which would still further destroy the past or pollute the future.

The large map shows the whole Peninsula whilst the smaller ones are designed to give the local information in detail and to provide some impression of the amenities which the visitor can expect to find. For information which is not from my own observation I acknowledge the research of Philip MacDougall in "The Hundred of Hoo" published by John Hallewell Publications and that of the late Brian Matthews in "A History of Strood Rural District" and published by the Council when it existed in 1971. Also Medway Military Research Group whose work is available in Rochester Public Library, Kent County Council's Footpaths Officers, and Officers of the Port of London Authority who taxed their memories for me.

Since the footpath along the sea wall encircles the Peninsula one might find it possible, by leaving private or public transport at selected places to traverse, on foot, a number of "loops" of varying length and interest to suit one's purpose and inclination. Access to Tide Tables may make a journey along the river side much safer and help to avoid disappointment.

D.S.W.

NOTES

The Suggested Walking Routes shown are over established Public Rights of Way as indicated on Ordnance Survey Map Scale 1:25000, Sheets TQ 67/77, Gravesend, and TQ 87, Isle of Grain.

Each Map of a Walking Route includes one or two of the places or objects or buildings in the collection of drawings.

The numbers inside the small squares are Kent County Council's footpath reference numbers, the other numbers indicate approximate heights above sea level.

TREES AND BIRDS OF THE PENINSULA

All of the Trees illustrated are either indigenous or, having been introduced some centuries ago, are almost as good as natives. All of them can be found on the Peninsula and especially in the Chattenden–Cliffe area which is the main area supporting timber growth. Some of the farms and larger houses have "exotics" in their gardens and they are worth looking at whilst passing with tree book in hand.

From among the several species of Oaks to be found, the Holm Oak is least frequently to be seen but there are good examples on Hoo Common, above Upnor and between footpaths 127 and 106. Holm Oak is evergreen and especially obvious in the winter. Incidentally, Holm means holly and this Oak is sometimes known as Holly Oak. The true Holly, Ilex, *is* a native of the British Isles and some good examples of it may be seen in the front garden of White House Farm, Stoke Road, Hoo, but there are others throughout our area. Apart from a few "skeletons" standing stark on the sky-line, the English Elm has disappeared as a tree but the suckers in the hedgerows are as prolific as ever and, hopefully, might become immune from the dreaded Dutch elm disease. The Horse Chestnut can be found but mainly in urban developments and cultivated places, and few can be seen East of Hoo. The Sycamore is ubiquitous and although of decreasing stature as it approaches the sea is especially noticeable in the Spring. There is Blackthorn in the fast disappearing hedgerows and copses. The same applies to Hawthorn but both of them, in the Northward Hill Nature Reserve, give shelter to the Nightingale. Poplars, in particular Lombardies, are extensively used as windbreaks and the Aspen, of the same family, can be found in thickets and other groups of trees probably planted to protect some of the farmhouses. Hazel, Birch and Beech are fairly profuse in the Chattenden Woods and there are some of each in Cockham Wood. There are several "singles" and groups of dramatic looking Pines — two such groups can be seen from the new Wainscott by-pass, to the North-West is

2

DSW.

Sycamore — acer pseudoplatanus

The Mount and nearer, to the South East at the Upnor Churchyard where there are five or six Austrian Pines, a close relative of the Scots Pine. The Yews in Hoo churchyard are worth more than a glance and there are a pair of "young" ones in the old school grounds, Stoke Road, Hoo, and similar ones at Cooling.

Several species of the bird population are of special concern to the conservationists and are not usually easily spotted and identified, but some, which can be seen after careful observation, whilst not uncommon, seem able to avoid the "spotter". From the latter group the drawings include the Nightingale (sings April to June), the Shoveller and Shelduck (river sides, mud flats, etc.), the Snow Bunting (Grain Flats) and Yellow Wagtail (Cliffe clay holes) and, of course, the Heron, which, having been deprived of the tall Elms has now settled for the sturdy Oak as a nesting place at Northward Hill.

3

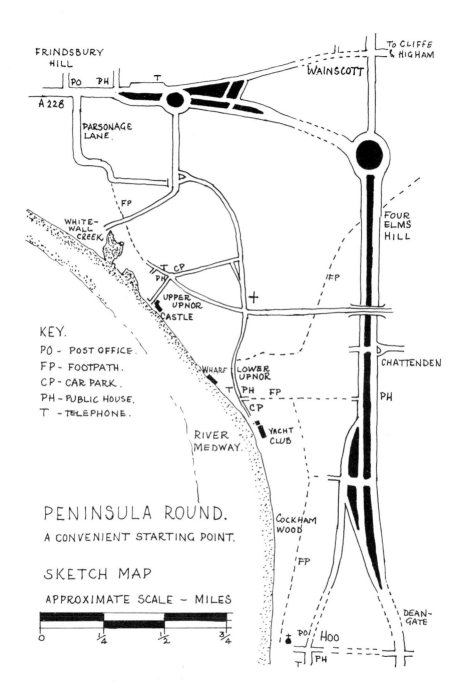

FRINDSBURY
HILL

PO   PH

A 228

PARSONAGE
LANE.

FP

WHITE-
WALL
CREEK

T CP

PH

UPPER
UPNOR
CASTLE

KEY.
PO - POST OFFICE.
FP - FOOTPATH.
CP - CAR PARK.
PH - PUBLIC HOUSE.
T - TELEPHONE.

WHARF

T

RIVER
MEDWAY

LOWER
UPNOR

PH   FP

CP

YACHT
CLUB

COCKHAM
WOOD

FP

To CLIFFE
& HIGHAM

WAINSCOTT

FOUR
ELMS
HILL

FP

CHATTENDEN

PH

DEAN-
GATE

PO

HOO

T   PH

PENINSULA ROUND.

A CONVENIENT STARTING POINT.

SKETCH MAP

APPROXIMATE SCALE - MILES

0   ¼   ½   ¾

4

S.S.Worsdale 1980

Manor Farm, Frindsbury

A good starting point for a walk, a cycle or car ride, is at the top of Frindsbury Hill (150 ft above sea level) and the sketch map shows the variety of directions from which a choice can be made. There is a 'bus service from the Medway Towns to the Post Office shown, and beyond it. Parsonage Lane is wide and little used nowadays and parking space is available.

The Administration and Legal Departments of Rochester upon Medway Borough Council are situated nearby and could be used if the need arose, in office hours. There is also a public telephone in the near vicinity.

The two Oasts and their setting behind the trees are an attractive façade for two more important and significant buildings which are not so readily visible. The Manor House is a late Georgian building on the site of a considerably earlier building. Fragments of Tudor work can still be seen. The Barn is an early medieval "Great Barn" and inside it some of the original cladding can still be seen.

Various alterations to the roads in this area have tended to "cut off" this little corner and scars on the landscape will soon disappear as Nature reasserts itself. Whilst here there is a good opportunity to explore the little used footpath to White Wall Creek and Upper Upnor. The Creek is the graveyard of several craft including Thames Barges.

High Street, Upper Upnor

DSW 1981

If one comes to Upper Upnor by 'bus (there are only one or two per week day) it might be thought better to disembark on the A228 at the Post Office on Frindsbury Hill and use the footpath as shown on page 4. Car drivers will find the Public Car Park the only sensible place to park, it's free too! The tall, slim weatherboarded and brick houses of the quiet High Street tend to remind one of similar streets elsewhere and where conservation is more obvious. But Upnor High Street has an atmosphere all its own perhaps engendered by that glimpse of the River Medway and Royal Dockyard at the bottom of the street.

Gazebo and Old Barracks, Upnor

The view above is best obtained with the tide "out" and the "hard" partly or wholly exposed. The old Barracks building broods over the scene including the prison like gates which are the main entrance to the Castle. The Gazebo is a well preserved novelty and makes worthwhile the necessary careful steps along the slippery hard to get the best view of it. Whilst it seems that the Castle was rarely, if ever, up to strength in armament or personnel, those who made up the garrison in 1667, when the Dutch sailed up the river, gave a good account of themselves in the battle which ensued and afterwards, doubtless, retired to the Barracks, bed-boards and palliasses.

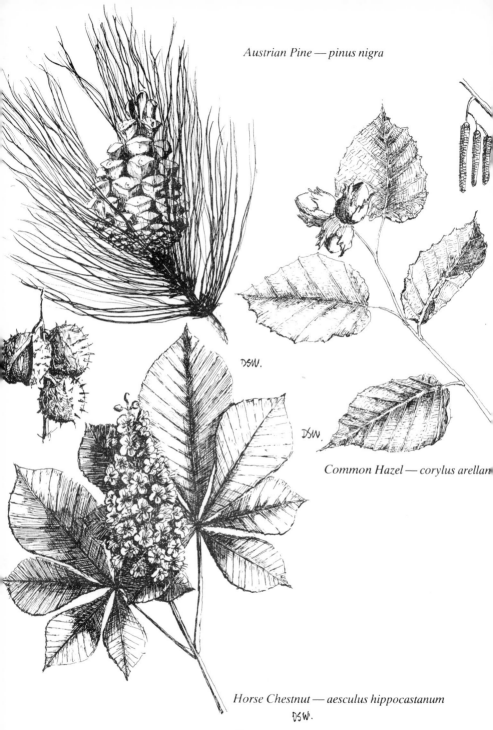

Austrian Pine — pinus nigra

Common Hazel — corylus arellan

Horse Chestnut — aesculus hippocastanum

DSW.

8

D.S.'vorsdale 1981

Upnor Castle

Queen Elizabeth I ordered that the Castle should be built. In 1560 Richard Watts of Rochester was appointed "Paymaster and Clerk of the Store" at two shillings per day. It had been proposed that, to save money, the stone from Rochester Castle should be used in the construction at Upnor. Watts resisted and new materials had to be used. In 1667 when part of the Dutch Fleet penetrated as far as Rochester its guns were engaged by those manned at Upnor. Samuel Pepys, writing in the days following the raid said "I did not see that Upnor Castle hath received any hurt". Of the gunners at the Castle he wrote "and they themselves shot until they had hardly a gun left". However the loss to our shipping was considerable and included the fighting vessels Royal James, Royal Oak and Charles V. The Royal Charles and The Unity were captured. The Castle can best be seen from the river but without a boat, a reasonable view can be obtained from the "hard", providing the tide is out. The great fence in front of the Castle is a current "Breaker" to limit the wearing effect of particle laden water in the tide's ebb and flow.

Incidentally Richard Watts founded a Charity in Rochester which is still flourishing today.

"Tudor Rose", Upper Upnor

This is another view of the High Street, Upper Upnor and gives, in conjunction with the drawing on page 6, an indication of the variety of domestic architecture which can be found here. It is partly authentic Kentish weatherboarding but there is also some brickwork which is bright red or is otherwise hidden in colour washes of pastel shades. "The Tudor Rose", was once known as the "Kings Head"; nevertheless it has an atmosphere which prompts the imagination. Across the road is the Gazebo and a large gate which consists in part of a Thames Barge Rudder. Upnor has two famous sons in Edward and Francis Pocock, young men of the village, who lost their lives serving with H. M. Stanley on one of his expeditions in search of the source of the Nile. Two of their souvenirs, an axe and a club, are preserved in Rochester Museum. The brothers were "Freemen" of the Medway and there is a memorial to them in Upnor Church. During the 19th Century prison hulks were stationed in the river at Upnor and not many guesses are necessary to establish the effects escapees might have had on the local population! Some assume that Magwitch (Great Expectations) was one of them.

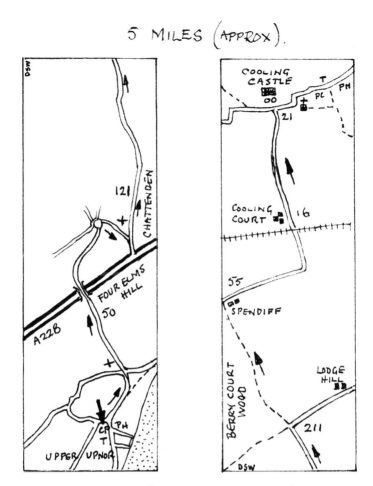

UPPER UPNOR TO COOLING CASTLE

From the map above the keen walker will see the possibility of an interesting walk of about five miles from Upper Upnor to Cooling and thence for a further three miles to Cliffe to connect with public transport. At about 500 yards after passing the bottom of the lane leading to Chattenden Farm one should note a military museum of enormous bombs and similar weaponry. Before entering Berry Court Wood and beginning the descent to Spendiff, why not consider a short climb to Lodge Hill from where, at about 240 ft above sea level, a splendid general view of the River Thames can be enjoyed? Unfortunately Lodge Hill House is now a heap of rubble. The house was built about 1760 and some of its occupants played a part in notable local events.

11

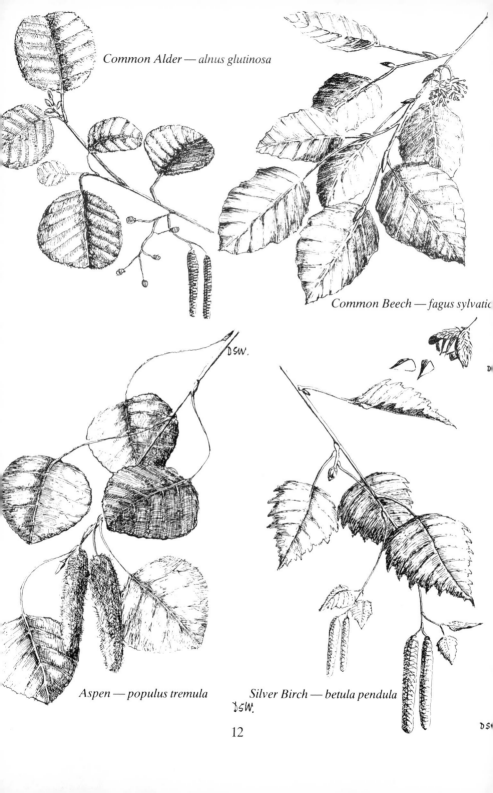

Common Alder — alnus glutinosa

Common Beech — fagus sylvatic

Aspen — populus tremula

Silver Birch — betula pendula

12

Figure-head at Venture Centre, Lower Upnor

Lower Upnor is noted for several reasons and perhaps the most commonly known is its association with Shaftesbury Homes and the "Arethusa", a four masted barque which used to be moored here. This vessel under its original name of "Peking" is now in a museum in New York. Nowadays Arethusa means a Venture Centre and a sloop which is frequently moored nearby.

The "London Stones" mark the limit of the fishing rights of the City of London. A stone at the mouth of Yantlet Creek marks the other limit. The smaller stone is thought to have come from Yantlet Creek and is dated 1204. The larger stone with several dates and names inscribed was visited in 1980 by the Lord Mayor of London at the renewal of an ancient ceremony not performed for 125 years.

As a Sailing Centre, Upnor has increased much in importance and from the London Stones it is possible to see at least three sailing or yachting clubs.

A footpath climbs the wooded hillside to the North and leads to the A228 at Chattenden. The visitor can go on foot to Hoo along the riverside, providing the tide is out. He will find the "going" rough but the passing scene of considerable interest.

The Five Bells, Hoo

Holm Oak — quercus ilex

14

Remains of Cockham Fort, riverside, Hoo

Cockham Wood Fort, such as remains of it, can be approached from Upnor or from Hoo, walking only. It was built, as were others, after the Dutch raid in 1667 and completed in 1700. It seems that no shot in anger was ever fired from its walls. It was expected to have towers and 50 cannon. Seventy years after its building, a Kentish historian reported that "all guns are dismounted . . . and the fort is becoming very ruinous". As can be seen from the drawing the remains of the casemates are visible. A tower and drawbridge with two flanking chambers, which stood behind, have long since disappeared. The construction is in mellow red brick.

Hoo St. Werburgh, known simply as Hoo, is a good starting point for walking. It gives its name to the whole Peninsula although historically St. James's and the Isle of Grain are part of the Hundred of Gillingham. Hoo is really a small town, well provided with Banks, Shops, Public Houses, Churches and Schools and a very good County Library. To the West of Hoo centre stands the Hundred of Hoo Swimming Pool. To the North of Hoo on the other side of the A228 is the Sports Complex, Deangate Ridge, Golf, Bowls, Tennis, etc. where food and Licenced refreshment is obtainable.

Holly — ilex aquifolium

English (or Common) Elm — ulmus procera

The Chequers, Hoo

The "Chequers" is one of the three pubs at or near the centre of Hoo. The "Chequers" and the "Bridge" are in Church Street. The "Bridge" is probably so called because it stands very close to a brook which passes under the road. The "Chequers" shown in the drawing illustrates well the Mansard roof which is a common feature of several buildings on the Peninsula, "pubs", farms or the larger dwelling houses. It is a typical country pub with a rural atmosphere despite its urbanised surroundings. During World War II, when many troops were stationed in the area and local amenities were stretched to the limit, the frequently overcrowded "Chequers" became known as the "Altmark".

St. Werburgh's Church, Hoo

The patron Saint is Werburgh, the daughter of a Mercian King named
Wulfere. But it was her cousin King Ethelbald who, to honour her, founded
a church and gave it her name round about 740. She had died in 700 and was
canonised shortly after. It seems she founded a nunnery at Hoo and for some
time her body was buried here until Vikings threatened the area and it was
removed to Chester for safety. So far as is known nothing remains of the
nunnery. The present Church is largely 13th Century on the site of an earlier
Saxon building. Various alterations were made and in the 15th Century, the
Spire and the stair turret were added. The Spire is 60 ft high and the only
remaining spire on the Peninsula.

Of interest inside is a stained glass window to Thomas Aveling (1882) of
Aveling and Porter who were first to produce the steam roller. In the
Churchyard is a tombstone to the memory of William White "murdered in
the bosom of his afflicted family" (1808) and thereby hangs a tale, an
unsolved mystery. The Yew trees are notable.

Barges at West Hoo Creek

The picture shows Thames Barges moored at West Hoo Creek (at this point sometimes known as Buttercrock Wharf). The breakwaters here and further upstream are provided by old concrete barges moored securely together. On the riverside of this anchorage or harbour is a concrete coaster, "Violette", which was launched at Faversham in 1919. "Violette" hit Southend Pier in 1921 and although declared a total loss served as a re-fuelling tanker moored just above Sun Pier, Chatham, up until, so far as is known, World War II. Anyone interested in Thames Barges can be assured, almost always, of finding one moored here.

Common Ash — fraximus excelsior

"Hoopride" at Buttercrock Wharf

D.S.W

It is quite surprising when walking round the corner of the shed on to the footpath on the sea wall to be confronted by the towering black hull of a coaster literally "up the creek". The small crane just visible over the gunwales has its base awash at some high tides. The coasters are owned by a local firm whose premises adjoin the shed. There is no special significance in the appearance of these coasters at Hoo but they do provide additional interest for the visitor and relate the present to the past which is so much in evidence with the barges, which are still working, and the "ribby" remains of others on the mud banks.

The footpath along the top of the sea wall proceeds in an Easterly direction from West Hoo Creek and is dominated by the tall chimney, some 600 ft, of Kingsnorth Power Station. The turbine hall is also prominent. Stretching out to the right (South) is the conveyor equipment terminating in the fuel unloading jetty. The old barge remains, not many left now, which lie like broken open skeletons, were probably used in making the defensive sea wall. Others are embedded in concrete or are filled with sand or soil, sturdy wooden walls still performing a vital function. If anyone is interested in old boat furniture such as batten hooks, fair leads and a variety of spikes and nails, the sand and wreckage should be searched.

St. Peters and St. Pauls, Stoke

Upper Stoke is one of three small units. The others are Middle Stoke and Lower Stoke. Upper Stoke has the Church of Saints Peter and Paul. It appears to huddle close up to a mound, or ridge, on the South side as if seeking protection from the bitter winds which blow across the river and the marshes. The main construction is 12th and 13th Century whilst the tower was added in the 15th. The tower was prepared to take a spire but it was never built, probably because the money was never available or perhaps because the Church would become too clear a landmark for the benefit of marauding bands approaching from the sea.

The East wall shows evidence of the damage caused by one of the 30 flying bombs or V2s which fell on the Peninsula during World War II. This was a V2 in June 1944. If your approach is from Hoo by the "low" road the first close view of the Church will be over a farmyard wall. Once, this view of the Church was obscured by a screen of Elms long since killed off by Dutch Elm Disease. Close by is access to Stoke Creek.

Court Farm, Stoke

Court Lodge Farm, also in Upper Stoke was once known as Parsonage Farm and appears as such on O.S. Maps until about 1958. This building is of the 18th Century. Before the name was changed, Court Lodge was to be found near to the access road to Stoke Creek. The Mansard roof is typical of several buildings in the area which recognise a French architect's skill in providing a garret with more head room. This is a good example, well maintained. The building to the left of the drawing (near the junction with the A228) is of interest too and one may surmise as to its intended function. There is one other such at Ridley near Meopham. The public house opposite provides parking space as well as refreshment.

Snow Bunting — plectrophenax nivalis

The Nags Head, Stoke

Remains of Grain Battery

The "Nag's Head" is one of several buildings in Lower Stoke with some claim to distinction. It was visited by the artist Hogarth in 1732 who, with four friends on a journey into North Kent (quite a safari in those days) found they had to share 3 beds between the five of them. It was an earlier building of course. It is reported that they complained later about being bitten by "gnats" (probably mosquitos).

In this village there is quite a large Methodist Chapel, built 1889, giving some indication of the popularity of nonconformity in the community. This building had a school room added in 1913 and has the "distinction" of being damaged in two World Wars. In the first by the "Princess Irene" explosion on the river and in the second by the V2 which also damaged the Parish Church.

If another diversion is sought, return to Middle Stoke, stop for a look at MacKay's Court Farm House then continue down the lane to Stoke "Halt" for another view of the Marshes. Some fishing water is nearby.

The Isle of Grain was separated from the Peninsula by Yantlet Creek. The village is really St. James's after the patron Saint. Nowadays we speak of Grain, meaning the whole "island" including, as well as the village, an oil refinery and a power generating station. In 1629 a visitor named Johnson described the area as "this barbarous country" but Hogarth and his friends (remember Stoke) had enjoyed themselves and they speak of passing through "this charming country". The Church is 12th Century, the porch was added in 1815 and the tower not until 1905. The door withstood the attacks of the Dutch in 1667. It is about 2 inches thick and the parishioners were able to find security behind it. The "Hogarth" Inn is named after the artist.

Shelduck — tadorna tadorna

Shoveler — anas clypeata

Blackthorn — prunus spinosa

Grain Tower

Situated at the confluence of the Thames and the Medway, Grain was an obvious place for defence works. Pass the Church, turn right, climb the slope and you will come to a deep moat; a few paces beyond is a deep hole with incongruous hand-rails marking the seaward side of it. This is Grain Fort, completed in 1867. A full complement of accommodation, magazines and lift shafts etc., are all now buried under an infill of rubble. Grain Tower, constructed in the 1850's, is situated on the edge of the deep water channel. Its base of stone and some of its masonry is 12 ft thick, the rest of the construction is of red brick and concrete. The causeway to it has tempted many a school boy to spend a complete tide cut off from shore, and from school, to the consternation of his parents. An unpleasant reminder of the last war is the sight of mast tops, well beyond the edge of the mud flats, showing above the water. This is the ammunition ship "Richard Montgomery" which sank near the end of the War loaded with various types of high explosive. The condition of the remaining cargo is monitored by Government Departments and other authorities concerned.

D.S.W

All Saints, Stoke

The Yantlet Creek prevents easy walking passage from Grain to Allhallows and it is much more convenient to return to Stoke via the A228 and from thence to Allhallows.

All Saints Church stands on a mound and the unusual Bell Turret will be seen first. It has parts which might be Norman but like most churches on the Peninsula is mainly 12th and 13th Century. The clerestory was added in the 15th Century, the porch and bell turret were added in 1890.

The public house across the road at the West end of the Church, the "Rose and Crown", is quite ancient and although its exact age is not known it is thought to have been a 16th Century ale house. It has had a variety of names but became "Rose and Crown" in 1841.

Slough Fort, Allhallows

For many decades Allhallows-by-the-Sea, as it has become known, was, and is, a haunt of holiday makers and week-enders. There are the usual holiday resort facilities. For cars there is an entry fee to the holiday estate (owned by the local authority) but there is a large area for car parking in an informal fashion. The view of the river and its passing traffic with the South Essex riverside as a backdrop, is always full of interest. Behind the car parking area is a steep mound which hides Slough Fort. It is an easy, usually breezy, walk along the sea wall to Yantlet Creek where there is a Beacon and a London Stone. The stone is significant since it marks the extent of the Port Rights of the City of London and the point from which fishing rights are claimed round to the stone at Upnor, also by the City of London.

Slough Fort hides descreetly behind a large hump of earth-work which rises from the riverside. It was built sometime after 1860 following a Royal commission into the coast defences when it was thought that invasion (by the French) was a possibility. Of semi-circular construction in granite it had armour plated casemates. It should have had 20 guns but finally only had ten, and then not until 1890.

During its life it was once a Zoo, but now is used to house a riding school. Its magazines are fodder stores.

FIVE MILES CIRCUIT

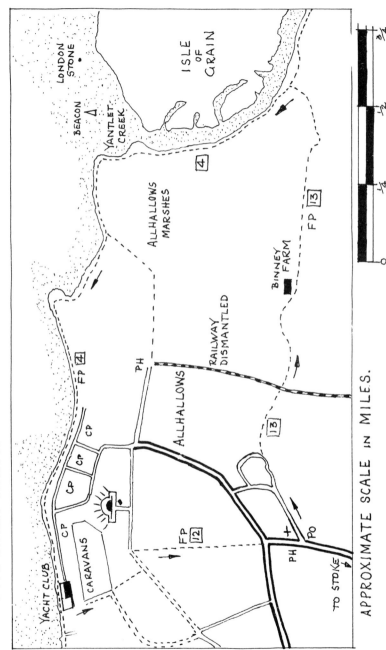

APPROXIMATE SCALE IN MILES.

Barn at St. Mary's Hall, St. Mary Hoo

St. Mary Hoo is nicely secluded and were it not for the Church its whereabouts would be even less noticeable. The picture shows a large, typical, barn and a glimpse of St. Mary's Hall. The Church is 13th Century and dominates a neat group of buildings; the village school (1868), the Hall, Red House, the Old Rectory and various farm buildings. Two names are noted in the village; the Rev'd R. Burt and Henry Pye. Robert Burt performed the "mixed" marriage of George, Prince of Wales to Mrs. Fitzherbert in 1785. He lived in the Old Rectory. Henry Pye lived at St. Mary's Hall and influenced farming techniques as to drainage, "chalking", steam ploughing and threshing in the late 19th Century. Newlands to the West and Coombe to the East are within the Parish. There are footpaths leading to Egypt Bay and St. Mary's Bay, old haunts of smugglers.

Common Yew — taxus baccata

31

DSW.   *Heron — ardea cinerea*

The Street, High Halstow

D.S.W.

DSW.

Nightingale — luscinia megarhynchos

The Street, High Halstow, is naturally come upon from the East, being a continuation of the footpaths and roads from St. Mary Hoo. Apart from St. Margaret's Church, Forge House (pictured) the "Red Dog" and the Nature Reserve are of note. Most local villages have some connection with the dim past through a personality and High Halstow is no exception. In 1450 John Clerk, the village priest, incited and led peasants and labourers to follow Jack Cade, who was campaigning for higher wages among other things. The Nature Reserve at Northward Hill, about 200 ft above sea level, is famous for its heronry and nightingales. About 400 yards along the Cooling Road a splendid panorama of marsh and river can be enjoyed. At this point one can easily imagine the days when, without a complete sea wall, small ships would quietly creep up the creeks and fleets for lawful and other kinds of activity. The straight line drainage system and the sea wall were largely completed in the 19th Century.

Cooling

34

St. Margarets & Red Dog, High Halstow

The Church of St. Margaret is not especially remarkable, being, like so many in the area, of 13th Century construction with 15th Century additions, mainly a tower. If a 16th Century map is to be believed there was once a spire, but, it seems, there is no other evidence for it. Campanologists might like to know that five church bells were installed in 1675 and in 1788 the bell-ringers claimed a record when they rang a five bell peal in 3 hours and 18 minutes. It is presumed they celebrated in the "Red Dog" afterwards.

The "Red Dog" is said to be of Tudor construction but it has been altered many times and rumour has it that more alterations are contemplated in this decade.

St. James's Church, Cooling, like St. Mary's at St. Mary Hoo, has no congregation now and is rarely open. Its earliest construction is 13th Century and the tower is 15th Century. Like St. Werburgh's it has a stair turret. Inside there are fine examples of medieval stone canopied stalls whilst outside are the well known lozenge shaped gravestones. Cooling is probably the smallest village, in population terms, on the Peninsula but with a considerable history. It is closely connected with the Cobham family and the artistocracy, although Jack Cade was well supported here and smugglers were familiar with the "lie of the land". The road from High Halstow twists and turns through rich farm land and neatly planted orchards, dropping down from 200 ft to about 10 ft at Marshgate House. This farm house is similar to several on the Peninsula. It is attractively situated and has an air of traditional stability and durability. By the way, the public conveniences here, just before reaching the Church, are a fine example of the standards which can be achieved and maintained by parish councils.

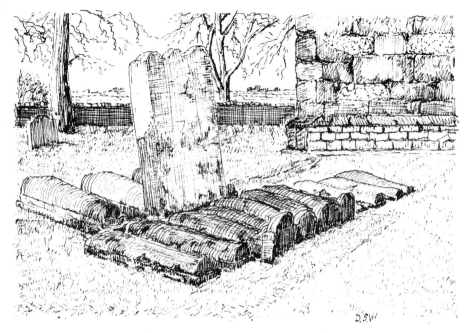

Lozenge shaped gravestones, Cooling

The lozenge shaped gravestones in the picture are 13 in number and of the children of the Comport family. All reference to the children suggests they were all under two years old at death. The cause of death was almost certainly marsh fever, or, as we now believe, malaria. One of the smaller upright stones is dated in the early 18th Century and this roughly coincides with the middle of a period of some 300 years during which the population of the Peninsula declined sharply. It did not rise again until the early 20th Century when positive steps were taken to control the mosquitos and consequently the incidence of malaria. The marshland is just over the wall and the Thames is but nearly two miles distant. The churchyard is about 20 ft above sea level and one can imagine swirling mists over the marsh and churchyard to the horror of villagers and parents of small children in particular over the centuries. Pip, in "Great Expectations", refers to lozenge shaped gravestones. Several villages claim they have the churchyard referred to in the Dickens novel and Cooling is a reasonable contender, but before conclusions are drawn, have a look first at the "setting" in the Churchyard of St. Mary the Virgin at Lower Higham.

Cooling Castle

A view similar to this one of Cooling Castle appears in most works about the area and is included here as a significant marker on the "Peninsula Round". The two towers are half "drums" — the two put together, back to back, would make one complete drum tower. There is a long history attached to the Castle but suffice it here to say that it was built in the 14th Century and, although time has ravaged its walls, it also suffered a battering by the cannon balls fired at it by Thomas Wyatt during the uprising he led in 1555 or thereabouts. It might be of interest to hear that Wyatt was besieging his uncle!

SIX MILES CIRCUIT.

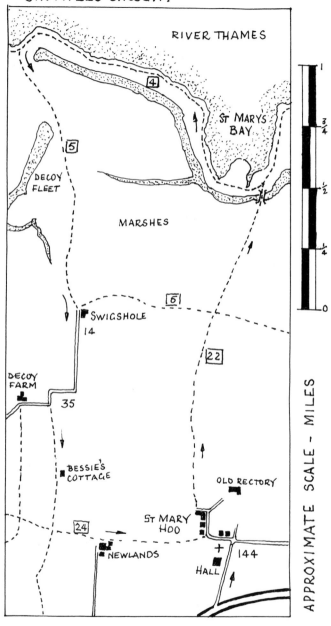

RIVER THAMES

St MARYS BAY

4

5

DECOY FLEET

MARSHES

6

22

SWIGSHOLE
14

DECOY FARM
35

BESSIE'S COTTAGE

OLD RECTORY

24

St MARY HOO

NEWLANDS

HALL
144

APPROXIMATE SCALE – MILES

1

¾

½

¼

0

Longford House, Church Street, Cliffe

The weatherboarded shops and houses in Church Street, Cliffe include Longford, shown here, which is an especially good example of "Kentish" weatherboarding with the overhang. Above Longford are cottages and shops which, together, create a 17th Century atmosphere. Opposite Longford is an arched passageway to the Church which is worth using for the sake of the view of the Church at the end of it. A convenient point at which to start a walk, or a ride, out on to the Marshes is down Church Street, and passing Courtsole on the left (and worth a look) turn right toward the lower end of Wharf Lane. Or, turn left below Courtsole and your journey can include the great Cliffe clay holes, and after a rough ride, reach Coastguard Cottages and the Thames River Wall.

St. Helen's, Cliffe

D.S.W

Weatherboarded shops, Church Street, Cliffe

Until recently these two long low buildings were used as shops and some living accommodation. It is not known what their future will be for what the picture does not show is that they are badly in need of repair and are probably very expensive to restore. Above and round the corner to the right (past the "pub") is an open space called The Buttway. It is an ancient recreation area for sport and games and archery practice. A three day fair is permitted under the authority of a 12th Century Charter. The School, overlooking the Buttway, was a National (Church) School built in 1854, about the same time as other village schools on the Peninsula.

St. Helen's Church may have some Norman origins but is largely 13th Century, with many additions including a double storey porch and a 15th Century tower. It is the only Church in Kent having St. Helen as the Patron Saint. The layers of ragstone and flint are familiar in this area. Inside, various architectural periods are clearly seen and the 14th Century South windows are of particular note. The remaining wall paintings indicate some of the magnificence of the medieval Church and are worth a moment's study.

Cliffe was at one time an important town and port but by the 16th Century it was in decline. The waterways were silted up, the sea walls decaying and the increasing incidence of malaria was persuading the population to move away. Several men associated with Cliffe brought it distinction, but one, Arthur Broome, a Curate at St. Helen's in 1812, called the first meeting (not at Cliffe) on 24th June 1824 which resulted in the formation of the R.S.P.C.A. Cliffe is a good place from which to take a close look at the Marshes. If descending from Allen's Hill take a look at the Tudor style chimneys of Manor Farm, West Street. Cliffe Fort, by the Thames, is worth a visit and the ever changing river scene is itself enthralling.

41

A CIRCUIT OF SIX MILES

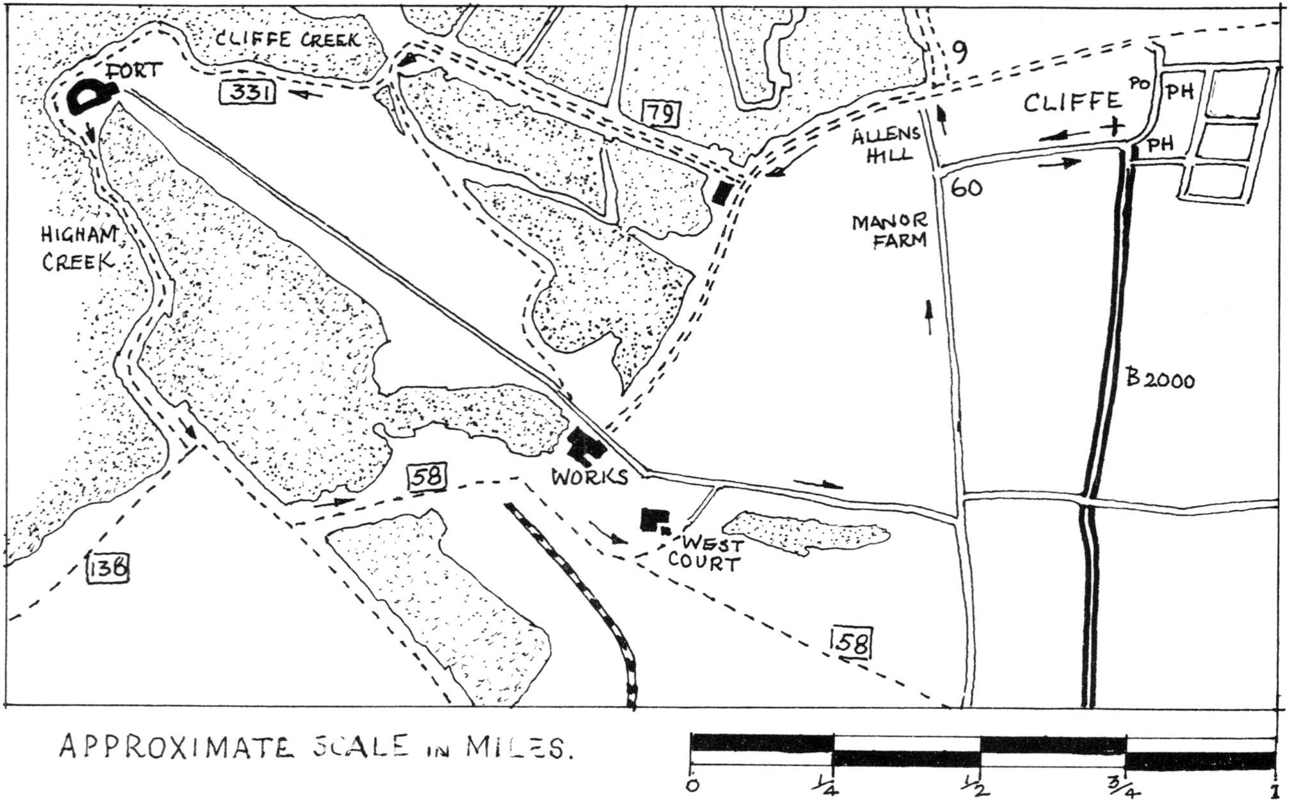

APPROXIMATE SCALE in MILES.

42

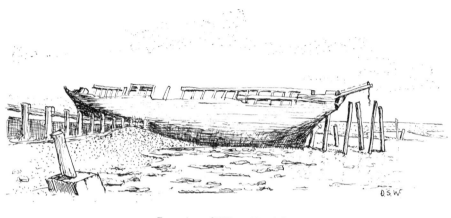

Remains of "Hans Egede"

With an interest in bird watching, photography, nature conservation or history there is reason enough for a walk beside the water filled clay holes below Cliffe. O.S. Sheet TQ 67/77 clearly gives the public rights of way in this area. An ideal point from which to view the river scene is at Cliffe Fort. The drawing shows the wooden hulk of a Norwegian vessel called "Hans Egede" which was being towed from Ramsgate to Thames for a refit when it sprang a leak off Egypt Bay and sank. To prevent it becoming a danger to shipping, some 20 years ago, Port of London Authority beached it where it now lies.

Cliffe Fort, near the hulk, was, like Slough Fort, built in the 1860's and its garrison was involved in experiments to develop the Brennan Torpedo which was never successful. General Gordon is said to have complained about fumes from a nearby cement works affecting the health of his troops and about a loading jetty being prejudicial to his plan for defence. Cliffe Fort was virtually abandoned in the 1920's but saw service again when a detachment of Home Guard ("Dads Army") was based there during the period 1939–1945.

Yellow Wagtail — motacilla flava

Thatched Cottage, Higham

Higham, it is usually agreed, is in three parts — Higham Upshire, Chequers Street and Church Street; or more recently as Higham, Lower Higham and Church Street. The latter is the smallest, the oldest and the most remote. There is to be found the thatched cottage shown, which is somewhat unusual, being larger and with a steeper roof than is common in the area. Further down the lane is another thatched cottage which is more in the traditional style but currently neglected. Beyond this cottage is the "Sun" with a deep pond a few yards from its front door — so beware! There are a few modern houses here too, but it is easy to cast the scene two centuries earlier.

St. Mary the Virgin, Lower Higham

The Church of St. Mary the Virgin in Church Street is on the site of a Saxon building. The North aisle is probably 12th Century or early 13th, and the difference between it and the South aisle, added later, can be seen by comparing, in shape and construction, the two East windows. The ragstone and flint walls are typical of the area, but the layering is not as precise as at Cliffe's St. Helen's. Inside the Church looks much larger than the outdoor view would suggest. Some of the wood-carving is 14th Century and will surely evoke the imagination of anyone who knows his timber and tools. The medieval carving and white oak of the church door are remarkable also. A brass plate in memory of one of Henry VIII's royal guards can be found here. The churchyard is still used for burials and like so many similar is overgrown. A glance toward the river across the marsh area may cause another thought about "Great Expectations" and prompt the question, *where* did Pip meet Magwitch? Rising from the roof of the North aisle is a short wood shingled spire which in its light grey colouring can be seen from far around. The site of a Benedictine nunnery is said to be in the vicinity, but it is only possible to guess its position.

Gadshill, Higham

Charles Dickens had a fairly long association with our area, walked its country roads and footpaths and undoubtedly visited Cooling, Higham and Hoo Churches. It seems that despite his early "delicate" constitution he later thought nothing of walking 12 miles or so at a "cracking" pace. He bought Gadshill Place in 1857 and lived in it for several months in each year until his death in 1870. Gadshill Place is now, appropriately, a school. The Chalet which once stood in the garden and in which he did a lot of his writing is in the garden in Eastgate, Rochester as part of the Dickens Centre there.

On the other side of the A226, Gravesend Road, the "Falstaff" Inn is a reminder of the days of highwaymen and such "brethren" who laid in ambush on the nearby hill. Telegraph Hill, behind the inn, provides an excellent view looking East and North.

Stone House Farm, Frindsbury

DSW '81

The "Peninsula Round" began with two Oasts and it seems appropriate to conclude with a similar number. Stone House is the Farm whose chimneys can be seen just behind the oast house in the picture. The public house nearby is the "Stone Horse". The buildings illustrated are not now used for drying hops for none are grown in the area but potatoes and other crops are now stored in them. The sight of three Oasts is a reminder that this is the County of Kent although the Peninsula is an outpost of it and has suffered isolation for about a century due to defence requirements and more recently due to industrial developments, which tend to discourage visitors, although they may cause an increase in population. Fortunately Kent County Council has now published a plan which, on the face of it, protects our present environment and designates sites of special scientific interest (S.S.S.I.).

DSW.

Common Lime — tillia x europaea

48